The Very Greatest Adventure

The Very Greatest Adventure...Is You Truly Being You

ISBN: 978-1-63493-280-6 (trade/paperback)
ISBN: 978-1-63493-281-3 (e-book)

For questions, please contact:
Access Consciousness Publishing
406 Present Street
Stafford, TX 77477 USA
accessconsciousnesspublishing.com

The Very Greatest Adventure

...is you truly being you

By The Being You Adventures

CONTENTS

WHY THIS BOOK?

There are no answers in this book.

No solutions to your problems.

No right road to follow.

Darn!

So why on Earth should you read it?

Well, this book is meant to remind you who you truly be:
a continuous creation.

Stop trying to find you.
You're not defined enough to be found, my friend.

Create you.
Choose you.
Be you.
Repeat.

You truly being you is the very greatest adventure!

WHO ARE WE?

In 2011, Dain Heer wrote a book called "Being You, Changing the World", an innovative toolbox for the seekers in the world.

Over the years, it has become so much more than a book... Today it is a class, a book club, a facilitators program and much more.

It is becoming a movement, a being you movement created by people's desires and demand to truly be them, to be the difference, to be more.

This book is a collection of ideas, perspectives and stories by the Being You Facilitators who are trained by Dain Heer and who facilitate *Being You Adventure classes* all over the world.

You will meet us throughout these pages, and if you would like to find out more, just go here: beingyouadventures.com.

What if you, truly being you, is the gift and change this world requires?

HOW TO USE THIS BOOK

1) Please know, there is no need to be linear with this book!

Start from the back, if you like.
Or in the middle.
Or just flip through and see what pages the universe desires to show you.
Grab a pen and start co-creating the book with us.

2) Maybe, allow it to just hang out with you for a few days?

- Have it resting and ready on your bed table?
- Or put it in the bathroom, if that is the place where you can find time for you?
- Or maybe in the kitchen, so other people can look at it while you bake them cookies?

"WHAT IF
NOT A DE
BUT A QUESTION,
A POSSI

EING YOU IS
FINITION,
CHOICE, A SPACE,
SILITY?"

—DAIN HEER

BEING YOU,
GIVING BIRTH

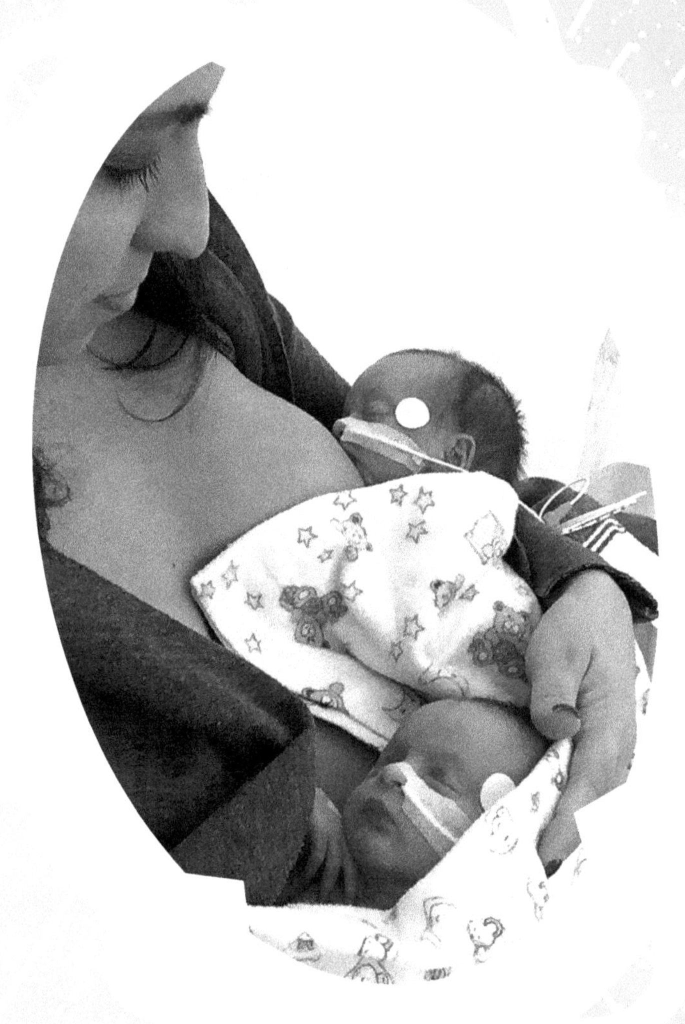

TWIN MAGIC

Lauren Marie, Australia

My water broke around one in the morning, seven weeks early. We were moving into a new house that day, or so we had thought. I tried to pretend it wasn't happening, but by 4AM I was having contractions and we rushed to the hospital. The twins had decided that was the day they were coming, and they were not stopping until they saw the world!

There were 18 people, including doctors and nurses, plus my husband all gathered in the room, just after 7pm, as I pushed those babies out. Nine for each tiny 4-pound little creature.

My daughter, Ayla, born first, was struggling to breathe, and they put her on a machine straight away. It covered her whole tiny face. My son, Preston, was born second, a bit heavier and more robust.

I begged to hold Ayla, and finally they consented, but they said only for two or three minutes, because she would need to go back on the breathing support. I held her tiny naked body against my chest, and I asked her to take anything she needed from my body and told her how much I loved her and that everything would be alright.

Almost immediately her breathing regulated on its own, and her heart rate stabilized. The doctors were so pleased to see the change that they let me hold her for over two hours in my wheelchair, chest-to-chest, where we slept. She never needed the machine for her lungs again after that.

I spent three weeks in that room, in a chair next to their incubators, tears streaming down my face. I saw them grow stronger and healthier every day. The tears weren't sadness, or fear, or worry. They were gratitude, awe, and amazement. I refused to leave their bedside, becoming slightly delirious from lack of sleep and nourishment.

They say there is nothing like the love you have for your own child. But I think what I experienced was actually something else.

We finally got to leave, nearly running out of that hospital, with our babies. I spoke to a close friend about how I spent the last three weeks crying, in wonder at the gift of these precious little ones. She said, brilliantly, "Welcome to being you."

I think it's like that for many of us, in these emergency situations, when we are called to be all of who we *be.* It was a space of such vulnerability and presence that I could not *not* be me. I had to, for the sake of these two lives, step into a space where I asked for—no—**demanded** that I do everything in my power to make sure they survived. Heart open, I was willing to ask for, and receive, contribution from every molecule in the universe and any willing hand outstretched.

I wonder what the world would be like if we could live that way all the time?

When I'm really being me, I am the space of being in totality that is literally connected to everything, includes everyone and yet it is also entirely me.

It has an immense space to it where my body is totally light without boundaries or stimulus. A vibrancy of being and body where nothing is tied, tight, diminished or limited.

—Tanja Barth, Germany

"TODAY YOU AR

TRUER TH

THERE IS NO ON

YOUER TH

YOU, THAT IS

AN TRUE.

ALIVE WHO IS

AN YOU"

—DR. SEUSS

The first time I discovered I was truly being me was when I heard music in the street and I started to dance with my entire body, without thinking about what anybody would say. That was courageous for me, and a moment when I was truly just being me.

To dance in the middle of the street in Turkey, in a country where everyone cares a lot about other people's thoughts and opinions, it was this moment that was the beginning of the change.

Now I do whatever I like and enjoy for me!

—Berna Sirin, Turkey

"LIVING IS T

OF EXPAND

THING IN Y

HE ACTION
NG EVERY-
OUR LIFE.'

GIVING UP CONTROL

Doris Schachenhofer, Austria

When I was pregnant with my first child, I was planning to have a home birth. Nothing else was acceptable for me at that time. My point of view was that birth is something natural, so there is no other option than giving birth to the baby at home and having a midwife.

The pregnancy was easy and relaxed. In the 7th month, the baby lay in breech position. The doctors told me straight away that I couldn't give birth to the baby at home and that I needed a C-section.

At first, I felt helpless and desperate about getting my baby two weeks before the calculated date of birth by C-section. I was calling my midwife and crying, asking her what else was possible, because this was not happening in my reality.

My main focus was to not have the baby before it was ready, and to be honest, to not have any injuries on my body. No marks, no cutting. My midwife found a hospital where doctors accommodate breech births. I got the consent to have the birth there, and my son was born naturally in breech.

I was always sure that my baby, and myself, would be fine. My midwife told me after the birth that normally women get cut during a breech birth, but this doctor did not, because he really perceived and acknowledged the capacities of my body. The birth took two hours.

This situation showed me that I cannot control everything the way I think it should be, but I can be in question about what else is possible. Giving up control and not holding onto the home birth opened up new possibilities that created so many more.

My favorite way to start being me again when I lose myself, is to allow myself to have a bad time and enjoy it. When I am done, I choose again, and to make it easier, I like to put on some good music or go out in nature, put my feet on the grass, lean against a tree, swim in the ocean and allow every molecule around me to contribute to and nurture my body.

—Susanna Mittermaier, Austria

Heather Nichols, USA

I had big, wonderful plans! I was going to have my sweet baby boy at home. In a big tub that my amazing midwife would provide. I had carefully chosen friends to be there, and we had everything perfectly planned!

On my due date, in the middle of the night, my water broke. It was time! This boy was coming. I called my midwife, alerted my birth team, and was all set!

Except… I wasn't having any contractions. And a few hours later, still no contractions. A day later, still no contractions.

When you have broken water, and no labor, you run the risk of infection to the baby. The medical world takes this very seriously, and would like to deliver the baby as soon as possible when this is occurring. Luckily for me, my midwife was brilliant, relaxed, and had delivered over 1000 babies all over the world, in many different third world countries, and often in 'sub-standard' conditions.

She kept checking the baby's heartbeat. It was fine. And I kept checking in, with my body, my baby, and my knowing. I knew it was ok. I knew he was ok. I knew we were ok. So we waited and did everything we could to get the labor started.

Three days later, still no labor; I decided it was time to go to the hospital and have my labor induced. We lied. We told them the water had broken 12 hours earlier, so they didn't pump me and the baby full of antibiotics. Still—I knew we were ok. We were actually GREAT!! And I just trusted myself and knew what I knew—beyond the intense fear of the medical world.

A little tiny bit of Pitocin later, and I was in full-blown labor. I insisted that I labor in the bathtub. I happened to have a nurse who knew my midwife well, trusted her, and let her take the lead, even though midwives are not allowed to deliver babies in the hospitals in my town. And my midwife let *me* take the lead. And I let my body take the lead, and show me what *it* knew about giving birth.

Apparently, my body knew a lot! I was not medicated at all during the labor, and rode the waves of the contractions with relative ease. It was the first time ever in my life that I had been so completely, totally, unwaveringly present for so long.

In one rare moment when I was anticipating the next contraction in dread, my midwife gave me some brilliant words of wisdom that apply to all of life: "Don't have a contraction when you are not having a contraction!"

I realized in that moment that, not only did my body know exactly what to do when the contractions were happening, but that I also could totally relax in between. I could allow my sweet birth team to pour warm water all over me. I could relax, I could be happy, I could be at ease, and I could receive.

I could ask for what I knew I needed, and allow everybody in the room to contribute to me and my baby.

When it came time to deliver, I got on the table and in a few sweet powerful pushes, Avery was in the world. My body knew exactly what to do. I never doubted it - and I trusted it, completely.

Once I was induced, it was a short four hours until Avery was in the world. The entire process was such a gift of trust, presence, potency, and me being willing to lead—the birth, the room, the people, the experience, based on what was true for me, what worked for me, what felt right for me, and what I knew also worked for Avery.

The experience of giving birth to this amazing boy changed me. I knew that I could trust myself like never before. And I got to experience the brilliance and the capacities of my body like never before. It was also the beginning of a beautiful communion between me and this amazing boy that goes beyond "mom and son," a true honoring of each of us, and one of the greatest gifts of my life so far.

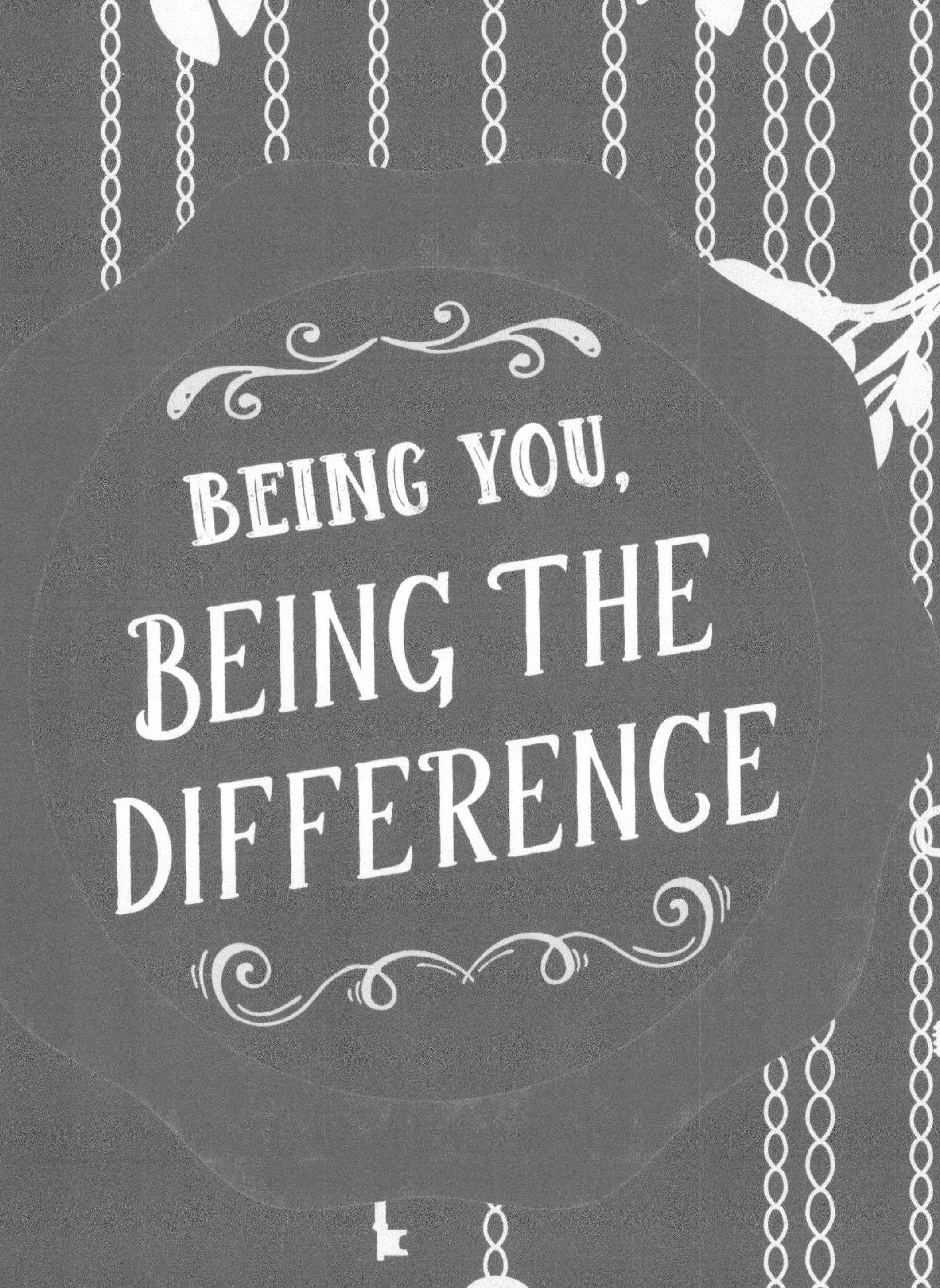
BEING YOU,
BEING THE DIFFERENCE

"WHY ARE
SO HARD TO
YOU WERE
STAND

YOU TRYING
IT IN WHEN
BORN TO
OUT?"

—IAN WALLACE

NO NEED TO PROVE

Stephanie Richardson, USA

The tricky thing about being you is that it doesn't feel like anything. Being you takes no effort.

"Do you think you have something to prove?" I heard someone behind me say.

I was interning for a global media company in the photography department, and I was carrying over a hundred pounds of sandbags.... It was my boss that had spoken from behind me. *"Yes!"* I replied. I did.

The photo industry is largely male dominated, and I wanted to prove that I could do what the guys could do on set. I didn't want special treatment. I didn't want to be looked over, or not be hired because someone thought I couldn't handle the job.

Always proving myself had taken a toll. I had begun to overlook that there were smarter ways that I could be working, ways I could do my job that would require far less effort and be way more efficient.

There was a handcart less than ten feet away. I could have carried 200 or more pounds at a time with a handcart. I could have chosen to take fewer trips and have total ease. Instead I was proving that I was "tough" and "strong."

By trying to be tough and strong, which is what I had decided must be valuable, I sometimes overlooked the other things that I had to offer; such as being smart, being efficient, being innovative, or even, *gasp*, being easy and fun!

What I didn't know, is that I wasn't being valued for being tough and strong at all. No one expected me to be tough or strong, except for me. Being tough was a job I had given myself. Unbeknownst to me, I was being hired for something very different.

A few months later, a very similar scene happened on another set... the photographer pulled me aside. "You know I don't hire you for the same reason that I hire the guys?"

I hesitated. I always wanted to be equal with the guys. What was this man saying? If I wasn't valuable in the way they were, what was I good for? I didn't want to be different. I just wanted to be great at whatever I did.

"You don't need to prove that you can do the stuff the guys do. I hired you because the set is really different when you're around."

What the bosses were trying to tell me, I didn't want to hear in the slightest. What they were telling me is that I was valuable to have around, not because I could lift over 100 lbs. of sandbags and not break a sweat, but because I was me. Having me around changed the way things on the set worked.

There would be many more times that I would still try to be what I thought I should be. I thought work was, by definition, where you tried to be what others wanted of you. I didn't understand that people would hire me to do what I do best, with the most ease, or even hire me just to have me around.

When I'm being me, I'm inspired, innovative, and a little quirky, easy and fun. Have you ever seen a little kid receive a gift they love and get really excited about it? That's what me being me is like.

When I'm trying to fit into what I think others want me to be, it requires that I look through the lens of what I think everyone else wants me to be. That's a lot of pressure and effort. Have you ever seen someone lifting really heavy weights? Have you seen the look on their face? That's the look of hard work and effort. That's what my face looks like when I'm not being me. Does it look happy, fun, and totally at ease? I didn't think so.

There's a strange ease in showing up and being you. You have a lot to contribute when you are being whatever combination of gifts and talents you are and contributing what you, uniquely, have to offer.

When using your gifts and abilities, you may feel like you're getting away with something, because work is actually fun. Or people may thank you for what you added to a meeting or a project, and you may find yourself wanting to say something like, "Thanks but I didn't really do anything... I just..." Most of us have no practice in having the life of ease that is being us and the gifts we are without effort.

The thing about you being you is that when you're most being it, you don't think about it. It's like your clothes. When your clothes are ill fitting, they constantly have your attention. You tug on them. You want to change them. You want to get out of them. When your clothes are comfortable, and you feel good in them, you don't walk around thinking about them all day; you just enjoy your day.

When you're being you, it's like being in comfy but sexy clothes! It takes no effort, and you look really good doing it!

I know when I am being me when I am having fun.

There seems to be a natural flow in everything in my day, from the creation of new ideas, my work, interaction with others, to how I handle everything that comes up.

There is also a different feeling in my body when I am truly being me; it doesn't even matter how much sleep I have had. I am full of energy and ready to create for the day. It's a space in which everything is possible, and a level of confidence in me where no one is going to stop me; including me.

—Laleh Hancock, USA

GRAB A PEN

WHEN WAS THE VERY FIRST TIME
YOU KNEW YOU WERE BEING YOU?

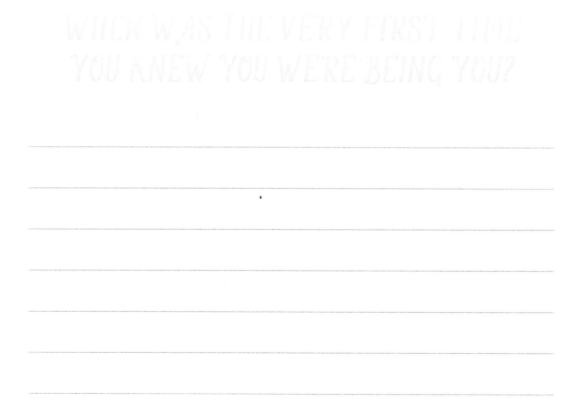

...IS YOU TRULY BEING YOU

Samantha Lewis, South Africa

I always thought I had to fit in. During high school, I was never one of the popular kids, I daydreamed a lot and missed most of what was taking place in class, except during art, history and geography.

I was fascinated by the evolution of things, of how people made things, how countries came into existence, and how cities were born.

I could never understand why my parents were so focused on test marks, when I was just happy getting the information. After all, didn't everyone see the pictures I did, or get a sense of those past times in history as I did? As I look back on my life in school and growing up, I realize that I thought everyone saw, felt and sensed things the way I did.

I would get confused when explaining something to a friend or my parents about what I was drawing or how I knew what my dog was asking for. They didn't seem to get it. They didn't get why, as a small child, I wasn't afraid of the big dogs at the end of our street; how I could pat them through the fence when everyone else walked away from them as far as possible. I would wonder if they knew what they were missing out on, how much fun it was to pat the dogs, and how grateful the dogs were for the affection.

I always had a sense of just going; keep going, don't stop! I had a lot of energy, and was always up early in the morning and the last one to go to bed. I could sit for hours on my own, reading, drawing, or just watching the trees in the wind. Everyone else always seemed to need something, to want to go somewhere. They seemed so far away.

When I finished school, I picked up the local newspaper and went for the first job that jumped at me and looked like fun. My dad told me I wouldn't get it, because I didn't know anything about it. I thought it was strange that he couldn't see the possibilities I could; that I could learn something new and that it was exciting to not know. I didn't realize then that the unknown, which was exciting for me, was frightening for most people.

My life continues, still with moments of, "Doesn't everyone see that? Or sense this or perceive that?" I now know that when I consider these questions, it's a moment when I can say, *"THIS is the gift of me being me — what I see, sense, perceive and know is unique and authentic to me."* I found the gift of being me, not by looking for how I am similar, or by hiding my differences behind a mask. I found the gift of being me in the ways I am different, in the unique way I create relationships, how I explore and see the world, and how I observe life and everything in it.

Being the gift of me is being this, nothing more, nothing less: just exactly this. BE IT, BELIEVE IT.

When I realized I could actually be happy, I just laughed and didn't stop laughing. I was 42 years old, and that was the first time I became aware I could actually be happy!

—Karlina van der Weij, Canada

"THE PEOPLE WH
ENOUGH TO
CHANGE THE WO
WHO DO."

ARE **CRAZY**

HINK THEY WILL

LD ARE THE ONES

—STEVE JOBS

Paulina Aguayo, Mexico

I have always enjoyed talking to people.

I remember as a teenager, talking with homeless people on the streets. They would come to me and tell their stories, and we would talk for ages. My friends would also come to me for advice or deep talks that I used to call, 'introspections'.

A few years ago, I had a fight with a friend who confronted me with her point of view that I talk too much, and that I go on and on, and that she and her friends were all sick of this.

In that moment, I had a sense of peace as I realized, "*Yeah! That's ME!*" I love to talk and share my awareness and experiences!

I acknowledge my choice of being me and their choice of being with me or not. So instead of changing for them, *I embraced all of who I am.*

HOW DO YOU KNOW WHEN YOU'RE BEING YOU?

I know I'm being me when I am relaxed and joyful, and when I see beauty and magic in everyone and everything I encounter.

—Kass Thomas, Italy

Bret Rockmore, USA

There is a capacity you have for creating change wherever you go.

You've always had it; you've always been it, ever since you came into this cute little body of yours.

Yet, for the most part, nobody has been able to see that.

Wherever you went as a child, people's barriers would melt, and their worlds became different, and yet the adults around you wouldn't even notice.

Then you started to learn how to talk, and your parents and society as a whole began to teach you how to fit in here.

They began to teach you everything they learned about how to survive here in an unkind world; they gave the tools they had been given.

And all the while you were trying to show them that it didn't have to be that way.

You tried sharing with them everything you knew that was beyond the reality that they had chosen to live.

And again, for the most part they didn't believe you. They told you, *"You can't do that. Be careful. That's not the way we do it here."*

Finally, you started to turn down and shut off all that you knew was possible, that they, unfortunately, could not receive.

Here is the thing: IT IS NOT LOST!

Instead you settled for normal, average and real.

You started coloring inside the lines . . . *to not upset the apple cart, to not be too much for other people to handle, to turn yourself down to make other people comfortable, to pretend to be what you are not, in order to make somebody else happy; and to tolerate that which actually does not work for you.*

What if you could un-learn everything that is keeping you coloring inside the lines?

What if you could invite back all of the parts and pieces of you that you chose to invalidate?

They've always been, waiting. It is you; it is who you truly be.

Are you willing to stop pretending to fit in?

Are you willing to be totally and unabashedly you, warts and all?

Are you willing to be too much and totally inappropriate?

Are you willing to start creating a life that works for you whether or not it makes your family happy?

Are you ready to start coloring outside of the lines?

HOW DO YOU FIND YOU, WHEN YOU LOSE YOU? THREE REMINDERS!

1. ______________________________

____

2. ______________________________

____

3. ______________________________

____

"NOBODY IS
ENOUGH
YOURSELF W

VALUABLE

TO MAKE

VRONG FOR.”

—DR. DAIN HEER

My quick and favorite tool to getting back to me when I have strayed is to lower all of my barriers, expand out as big as I can, take a deep breath (or four) and ask, "*If I were truly being me right now, what would that be?*" And then, from that space, proceed with my day. Oh, and repeat as often as required!

—*Gabriella Vena, USA*

Simone Arantes, Brazil

I grew up in total wrongness, basically believing that every single part of me was wrong.

I did not fit into most people's points of view on how things should be, or what and how I should be.

When I was about to choose what to study at college, I talked to my dad and said, *"I would like to be a judge."* He told me that I couldn't be a judge, as there were no women at the magistracy. But, he said, I could be a lawyer.

As I did not desire to be a lawyer, I decided to study chemistry, and I went on to receive a PhD and a Post Doc in Chemistry. However, despite that accomplishment and the ease of which I achieved it, I never acknowledged any of it.

I just continued to live my life, never truly happy, never really feeling like I succeeded with anything. It was not until later that I realized, while I was talking to my dad that day, *I had chosen not to succeed.*

That was life changing for me.

It showed me that nothing ever just happened to me. I have chosen (although not cognitively) every single thing in my life. After realizing that, I have now started to choose everything in my life. I have chosen to be as weird and different as I truly be, whether or not people judge me.

My life is a gift to me now, and I am the one who has chosen it.

HOW DO YOU KNOW WHEN YOU'RE BEING YOU?

I know I'm being me when I laugh without having an excuse, and when everything is easy and fun and amazing!

—Claudia Cano, Mexico

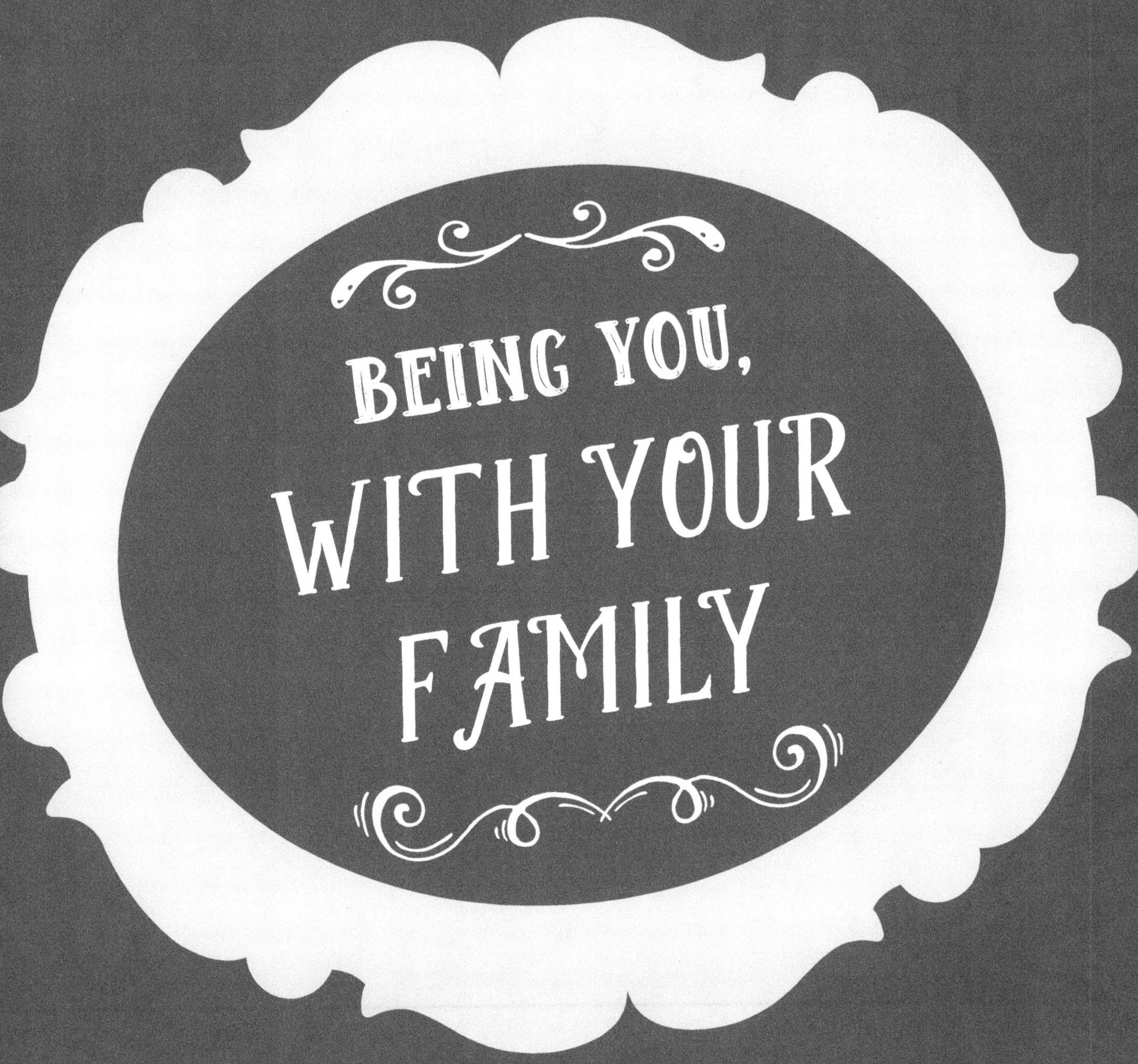
BEING YOU,
WITH YOUR
FAMILY

Shivam Saxena, India

Very early on in my life, I realized I was not like the mean, abusive, violent, manipulating and dominating family I was born into. I needed no proof; I just knew I was not like that. I was probably six years old, and didn't know all my alphabet, or numbers beyond 50, and yet I knew I was different.

I used to wonder who I really was.

My parents were adamant about respecting elders, to the point where our family was like a hierarchical command system. My elder siblings had the right to bully me, and I still had to be respectful.

Being the youngest, and also a girl, I had no voice, no right to choose for myself, and no value at all. In the face of horrendous abuse, and no support from anyone, I taught myself to have my own back. Each time I delved into, *"If I am not like them, then who am I, really?"*

Layer by layer, I started to discover a new aspect of me, and a whole new level of strength showed up.

The crazy part is that each time I was armed with more of me, people backed off; more change showed up, along with more space for creating my life. The choice was clear to me; either look at what more was available to me and show up as me - more and more - or go down the gutter with the rest of them.

By the time I was eleven years old, I was done with the physical and sexual abuse I'd been facing at home. I searched online and found a boarding school in the south of India that I really liked, and that had a headmistress that I thought would hear me.

The next day I wrote her a letter in which I was totally vulnerable. I wrote to her, *"I am not very good at studies, and here are my marks..."* Then I explained to her the real reason why I wanted to leave my home.

This was one of the top 20 schools in India, where children from all over the world attended. I had no clue about what an application fee or the process was. I just wrote that letter. A couple of months later, I got a letter back from the head mistress asking me to come with my parents to appear for an interview.

So, there I was — first step accomplished. Now, it's amazing how the universe conspires in favor of you when you commit to you!

My parents were initially very reluctant to send me away, but my father had a very senior position with the Indian government and was posted in a very crime sensitive area. Just around this time, he had received a police report of terrorists planning to kidnap me.

They basically had no choice but to ship me off to a safer location, and what better place to send me to than the boarding school I picked? *Thank you universe!*

For me, that creation at eleven years old is a huge testimony to what you can create when you commit to yourself. You will not just survive or get by. You will thrive. And this was just the beginning . . .

When you choose to *truly be you*, you don't have to buy the shenanigans, the lies, the dogmas, the fears, diseases and sickness of people around you. You put a stop to the limitation your family can be.

When you choose to truly be you, you can actually create a life that is true for you, beyond the people or family you are born into.

HOW DO YOU KNOW WHEN YOU'RE BEING YOU?

I know I am being me when I have a sense of a space of no judgment around me. When I am not in reaction, or the effect of anything. When there is ease and I am happy for no reason. When I am grateful for everything, and it is so much fun to be alive. During this time, I know everything is changeable and that I live from what is possible, rather than from the limited points of view of other people.

—Margit Krathwohl, Germany

"IT IS NOT O

THAT SHOW U

IT IS OUR

R ABILITIES

WHO WE ARE.

CHOICES."

—DUMBLEDORE *("Harry Potter and The Chamber of Secrets")*

RECEIVING YOUR FAMILY

Susanna Mittermaier, Austria

Growing up as an only child with sweet parents who made me the sole center of their universe, I learned to be very aware of people's needs.

At some point, around my teenage years, my answer to being two people's whole universe was to protect myself. I thought I would disappear, and my very being would cease to exist if I did not put up walls and barriers to maintain a sense of self.

I even perfected that whole maneuver by creating a comfortable distance from the whole world. As long as I had that barrier up, I could make sure that I would have me. Or at least, so I believed.

If you in any way recognize yourself in reading this, it may be time to ask yourself the same questions I finally asked. *"Does that really work? Is this really giving me the life I would like to have? Does this really bring me joy?"*

You know the answer to this, don't you? It blew my whole world apart and shattered the barriers that I thought were my best friends, my brothers and sisters. In that moment, I knew they had to be let go of, if I wanted to have the freedom and the space to be me.

A good friend of mine said, "*What if you just receive what your parents are gifting you? What if you let that in? It does not matter what it is — if you receive everything and don't judge it anymore, you will always have you!*" No one can take you away from you, if you don't let them.

I realized how much we judge what is being directed at us and then put that in boxes with the labels, *"good energy, bad energy, I like, I don't like."*

I remembered when I was a kid, when I was grateful for every word my parents were saying to me. I know that sounds a bit weird, because it is weird in our world to have that level of gratitude for each other. By the time I was a teenager, that gratitude was gone, in favor of separating from them in order to find me.

So . . . I asked to be that again with my parents and let them in. Since then my world has completely changed. Not only do we have so much fun with each other, but that choice allowed me to receive the whole world in a different way.

I now know that I *am* the world, and that we can all be with each other in a totally different way once we choose to lower our walls and barriers.

Yes, we are sometimes met with particular energies and people we think we should not receive, because if we did, they would destroy us. But, what if this is the biggest lie you have ever bought!? What if receiving them would give you, *you*? I know it did for me, and does every day. Is it worth a try?

[illegible] I WAS REALLY BEING ME

People, things, situations that were seemingly unchangeable before, magically changed. The impossible, became possible. Just by me, *willing to be me*, people were inspired to see; all of that was also possible and available for them to choose, if they desired it. They were grateful to realize that it doesn't have to be hard, and it is just a choice.

—Marja Zapušek, Slovenia

Pam Houghteling, USA

Throughout the years, I've discovered many tools about being you that I also introduced to my husband. Through them, we let go of many of our points of view about marriage: what it meant to be married and the projections, judgments and expectations that go with it.

Living together and creating our lives together was a choice we made every day. Now and then in the 20 years of our relationship we had, "state of the marriage" talks to ask questions about what was working or not working about being married, and what would we like to change.

One night after I returned home from a seminar, we again asked questions, and for the first time it felt lighter to not be married than to be married. We asked even more questions, and in the course of a five minute conversation, we chose to no longer be married.

We then talked for an hour and a half about *how* to separate, including what to tell people. We knew it would be easy to create problems that were not real, as people would look for a reason for why our marriage was ending: **That a marriage can end by choice is not really something people have an easy time accepting. Yet.**

We had a very good time over the next couple of months implementing our choice. We were each being and choosing what was going to create greatness for our family. There was no judgment, no anger, and no problems. We continued to be very good friends and we contribute to each other and enjoy each other.

I know this is not how it works in 99% of marriages that end in divorce. I also know that it could be!

If I am laughing, dancing, skipping or running, it's a good bet that I'm being me.

—Lauren Marie, Australia

"CHOOSING Y
IS THE GREAT
CAN GIVE TH

OUR REALITY
EST GIFT YOU
E WORLD."

—DR. DAIN HEER

It's so obvious when I lose myself. My head pounds, my body is sluggish, my awareness is numbed, my consciousness dense. Ugh, what a struggle!

As soon as I sense any or all of this, I ask, "*Who does this belong to?*" Then I stand up and place my hand on my heart center (thymus) and the other on my lower abdomen (public bone), close my eyes and breathe through my mouth. I expand my energy to the four corners of the room or space I am in. I ask the Earth to contribute to me and expand me beyond the density and heaviness of the reality I got stuck in. Then I expand as big as I can imagine, bigger than the universe, earth, sea and redwood trees I marvel at regularly.

I then dissipate the energy to the earth by imagining it fertilizing the earth and generating a new possibility. This leads me to a renewed sense of me and frankly right back to be the generative possibility magnet I truly be! It is with this practice I know that I matter, I exist and I roar!!

Dr. Lisa Cooney, USA

ANGER, LOVE AND EMOJIS

Hanna Valdevi, Sweden

I was in the middle of a business meeting when my 9-year old son called me on his way home from school to ask me for something. When I didn't agree and didn't reply yes to what he wanted, he became very angry, screamed in my ear and hung up on me while I was still talking to him.

My reaction to this surprised me. I got very upset, embarrassed and angry—and at the same time tried to keep my face on in front of the people in my meeting. It didn't get better when my son started to express his anger by sending me text messages every ten seconds; text messages filled with angry emoji faces. I had a hard time concentrating on the meeting.

As the anger kept building within me, I tried to figure out how I could take control over the situation, so I could go on with the meeting without totally losing my appearance as a business professional.

In a very "adult" way, I started to write an angry text to my son, while at the same time, I got more and more contracted and disconnected from myself. Halfway through my angry text, I couldn't help but laugh at myself and my reactions. Who was I being in this situation? What was I trying to prove, and to whom? And what energy was required to change all of this with ease, for both me and my son?

I realized I had learned at an early age that hanging up the phone on someone was disrespectful and something that you should be very upset about. And when I was angry as a child, one of my parents defeated that anger by directing even more anger towards me.

So, whose point of view was this really? The contraction in my body was a good indication that it surely wasn't mine. I asked myself, *"If I would truly be me in this situation, what would I be?"*

A totally different energy became very present in my body, and suddenly I had a smile on my face. My body relaxed. I erased my angry text lecturing my son and instead replaced it with emoji's, reflecting the new energy that had shown up and sent it to my son.

This photo is a screenshot of our conversation that day.

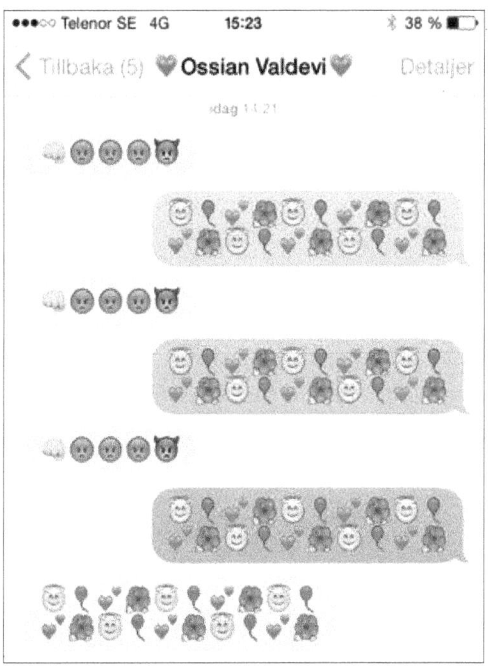

When I shifted my energy, and got rid of my points of view about anger and me as a parent, I became more of who I truly am, and it took him 30 seconds to change.

I was amazed, and so were the people in my meeting. What if you, being you, is all that is required to change any situation?

BEING YOU,
WITH YOUR
BODY

Susanna Mittermaier, Austria

When I was working in mental health as a psychologist, I met patients who were staying at the psych ward for weeks, and sometimes even months.

The ward was an old building with plastic floors. The interior design was as uninviting as a train station. Combined with people who were at the lowest point in their lives, it was a place that was not designed for any healing or nurturing.

Since I had a full-time job and had to be there many hours of the week, I asked myself, "*What is possible here? How can I make this as easy and nurturing for me and the people I work with?*"

At that particular ward, the staff did not wear uniforms. We could wear our personal clothes. We did not have white coats. My colleagues usually dressed in "working clothes" like jeans and T-shirts.

My point of view about clothing is to always pick what makes my body happy, independent of the occasion. So, I asked every day, "*Body, what would you like to wear?"* Most of the time, it was nice dresses, high heels, and nice jewelry.

I asked my body, *"Are you sure? We are going to work." "Yes!"* was the reply. At work, my colleagues used to tease me by asking, *"Are you going to a party?"* to which my reply was, *"This IS the party! If it is not, why be here?"*

After some weeks of me working at that ward, one of the patients peaked out of her room and said, *"Susanna, come!"* She waved and invited me into her room.

This was a woman that had been at the psych ward for weeks. She had actually been in and out of the psych ward since she was a child. Doctors had pretty much given up on her. She existed, but was not much alive. She had attempted suicide several times. One time I found her lying in bed, in a blood bath. She said so many times that her body was her prison and that she wanted out.

This day, when she invited me into her room, she had a light in her eyes that I had never seen before. She stood next to her closet and asked, *"Susanna, can you help me? You always look so pretty. I would like to look pretty today too. Do you think that this shirt goes with these pants?"*

Wow! I could not believe what I had just heard! That woman had never cared about her body for as long as I had known her. Getting her to take a shower was a struggle. And here she was with a desire to honor her body and to care for herself in a way she never had before!

And it did not stop there. Days and weeks thereafter, patient after patient started to dress up and ask about styling tips. If there had been an award for best-dressed ward, we would have won it!

This sounds like a little thing, but it was a huge step in these people's lives to include their bodies, honor them and make a step towards the choice to live.

You never know who you'll inspire by choosing to be you. It may surprise you in what ways you can actually inspire the world and people around you.

And often it is the very things that are so easy and normal to you that you don't even think about them . . . *Your difference is changing the world, right now.*

A lot shifted for me when I started being more of who I truly am. Suddenly, I was interacting with more people. Friends, as well as strangers, would literally stop and ask me what I was doing different to look and be so happy all of the time. I started choosing things that were fun for me instead of being at the effect of other people's projections.

More than that, I realized that something I'd made myself wrong for throughout my life, my kind and caring nature, was actually my strength. This is what helped me heal and create maximum changes in people's lives.

I realized that doing something from the joy of it created so much more than just looking for perfection.

—Smriti Goswami, India

"MOST PEO
NO IDEA H
THEIR BODY
TO FEEL."

LE HAVE

OW GOOD

IS DESIGNED

—Kevin Trudeau

Betsy McLoughlin, USA

Have you ever felt disconnected from yourself and your body? Well, I have for most of my life!

I have judged the heck out of my body, in every different size I've ever been - from a Size 14 to barely fitting into Size 32 Woman's clothing. I judged myself into severe depression and got to the point where I was contemplating suicide. I also had several illnesses, including cancer

Without realizing it, I had exiled myself from me. I had literally erected huge, thick walls around myself with my larger body size as well as emotional walls far larger than I could imagine.

I had no idea who I was. I did have glimmers of happy, fleeting moments of me—only to lose myself in the black hole of never ending self-judgment, self-hatred and body abuse.

After many, many years of spiraling more and more in the mire of this self-imposed exile, I said ENOUGH!

I was so tired of body pain and hearing myself complain all the time. Something had to change, or I really did not want to be on this planet anymore living the life I was living

Have you ever noticed that when you make a demand for something, opportunities start to show up to contribute to your request? The universe is kind of brilliant that way—if you ask! I started to see possibilities where before I had only seen dismal despair.

One day a friend told me about Access Consciousness Bars, and this two-minute conversation changed my life. Access Bars are 32 bars of energy that run through and around your head that connect to different aspects of your life. Lightly touching these points begins to clear away the energy locked there. When these points were touched, I was amazed at how I felt, simply from having my head touched! After my first Bars session, I had peace and calm, no constant judgment chatter in my mind and I was happy! This was the beginning of changing my life that I had demanded show up.

Since then, I've had my Bars run as often as possible—when it's been too long, my body asks for a session. I start to get headaches, or I feel crabby. As soon as my Bars are run—BOOM — I'm ME again and the headaches and the crabbiness disappear.

I continue asking for more communion with my body, more ease in my life, and guess what? It is showing up in delightful and fun ways!

I am no longer hiding who I am. The constant self-judgment of my body size is gone—no matter what size I might be that day.

That release of judgment has unlocked everything that I was hiding behind the thick walls. Now, I am able to embrace all of me—my beautiful imperfections and celebrate everything I've created!

I am grateful for the journey; all of it has contributed dynamically to my life.

I'm here to tell you, my friends, that it is totally possible to change your life if you desire something different! I encourage you to ask and see what shows up for you!

If the Queen of Self-Judgment can become herself and banish judgment—*so can you!* You can create the life you desire my friends!

I know I'm being me when a feeling of joy and happiness rises inside of me that I feel throughout my cells. And in that moment, I know that I can succeed in anything and can create everything. It is not about HOW. It is just BEING.

—Berna Sirin, Turkey

GRAB A PEN

HOW DO YOU KNOW WHEN YOU'RE TRULY BEING YOU?

...IS YOU TRULY BEING YOU

Angela Kovacs, Hungary

One morning I woke up in deep pain. It had happened so many times, especially when it would rain during the evening, so I was not that surprised. It seemed worse than normal though.

It always took an hour to warm up my joints before I could go to work . . . And when I got there, I did not allow myself to suffer from my own pain. Instead, I listened to other people's problems.

This particular day, I took the usual bike road to work.

The wind was blowing in my face, and I became more relaxed.

Then, a leaf fell in front of me, slowly. Time just stopped. The space expanded. I was laughing like crazy and crying at the same time over the leaf that had landed on my bike.

It seemed like this brief moment lasted an hour.

And this one leaf inspired me to move towards something else, towards a different energy, a different space, a different everything.

It changed my day, my world, and gave me the message that there is something else available here. I am not alone.

There is contribution all around us.

If every simple moment and every leaf can be such an invitation, what else is possible then?

If every molecule can be such an invitation, what else can we ask, receive and create in the future?

I have a simple four-step process for finding me when I'm lost.

Step 1. Notice that I'm lost.

Oh, I'm chattering away in my head again, replaying a story from the past, or worrying about the future. Or, I'm feeling heaviness or tension in my body that wasn't there a moment ago. Or I'm behaving in some bizarre way, or judging, or saying something that isn't my point of view.

Step 2. Choose

OK, I'm lost. Would I like to change that? Sometimes, I really want to finish telling myself that story again, or to indulge in the heaviness or tension or confusion that isn't mine. That's okay. I'll check in again in a few minutes.

Step 3. Ask

Open-ended questions are like a magic compass pointing to me. Like these questions, "Who does this belong to?" "Who am I being?" "What's right about me that I'm not getting?" Questions help bring me to the present and create space for a different possibility. They invite me to notice what is true for me. Instantly, I'm back with me and my body, present and aware of the moment, and being me. And it's the most beautiful sensation.

Step 4: Acknowledge

Now, I notice what it's like when I'm being me. I acknowledge the choice I've made to be me, and the change I've created. *Hi, me! I'm back!*

— *Kristen Tromble, Alaska, USA*

"If you do not stop, you cannot fail."

—Dr. Dain Heer

I know I am being me when I am full of joy. I do not necessarily need to be loud and outgoing. It is the space of joy where I am not reacting or fighting. Being me is not stepping away from what I know, even if it is uncomfortable for others, or even for me.

—*Doris Schachenhofer, Austria*

MY MUDDY PRINCESS

Doris Schachenhofer, Austria

My daughter allows herself to be the princess, as well as the girl that gets muddy. I can watch her being all of her all of the time. She inspires me.

I watch her changing situations within seconds. She is talking to everyone everywhere. She meets people and just says "hi", and their worlds melt from whatever they were experiencing in the moments before. The ease she has with being her is such an invitation that we can change every moment in our lives to something greater if we choosc to.

She is joy embodied, and she wants everyone to know that life can be fun.

She is five years old now, and I have to say that I have often dismissed her invitation and have just been annoyed when she arrives to change the situation. Now I can receive it more, and I have such gratitude.

What I love the most is that she shows me that she has absolutely no point of view, and that nothing is relevant for long. Sometimes I apologize for what I have said to her, or how I've acted around her, and she replies, *"Everything is fine mum."* After that, she turns around to go on.

It astonishes me every time, and it is such a gift to me to not judge me, and to look at what else is possible and what else I want to choose.

She is definitely changing my world by being her.

If I am really being me, I am spacious. You may ask, "*What the heck does that mean?*" For me, it means I don't sweat the small stuff.

When I am spacious, very little is significant or seemingly important. I wake up happy and with gratitude for the birds singing, or the color of the clouds before sunrise, or the light in the room when the sun just peeks over the mountains.

This pervasive gratitude is a sure sign for me that I am being me.

—*Corinna Stoeffl, Germany*

“LIFE IS A
CHOICES,
CHOICE Y
MAKE

MATTER OF
ND EVERY
OU MAKE,
YOU."

—JOHN C. MAXWELL

Laura Simmonds, United Kingdom

Being a single mom with three beautiful teenage daughters can be challenging. And yet I now have a lightness with it that still surprises me at times.

I remember when I first noticed that there was simply an ease to it all that had never been there before. It was about two years ago. At first, I put that down to their age, justifying it as a new phase with older and more mature children. *What I didn't acknowledge at first was the change I had chosen to BE.*

Before that, I remember looking at my life and questioning all of the things that weren't working for me. My life had been mostly all about everyone else's happiness. Somehow, I had convinced myself that I, the strong, independent one, didn't really need to be happy. In many ways I didn't even matter at all—I just wasn't a priority. I was a MOTHER after all, and if they were all happy, then I was happy

I woke up early one morning as the sun was rising and the dew was still fresh. I went for a walk in the beautiful countryside where I came across some rabbits in the field beyond. Some of them were playing, whilst others were grazing in the quiet undisturbed path ahead.

As I stopped to watch them, I looked and noticed that each one was doing what each one wanted to do, and that between them there was a sense of ease of just being together. «What was that?» I asked myself. "*What are they being that we are not?*" I started to ponder.

And then I knew; a word just flew into my world and lit everything up like a beacon: ALLOWANCE!

That was the moment when everything started to change, and being a mom became more ease and joy, rather than a challenge. It was the moment I started to question everywhere I didn't have allowance for me, everywhere I didn't have allowance for my children and everywhere I wasn't including ME. From that space, I demanded a change.

It was the moment that I chose something different: *I started to include me in my choices.* I began to choose for me, for my happiness and for my being. And in doing that, I started to see with my own eyes, the change and the beautiful gift that is.

It was like a magic wand spreading a warm and radiating light to everyone around—including my daughters. They started to choose that too!

I noticed that I didn't actually have to DO so much in order for others to be okay. It really was simply enough for me to **be me.**

The way I know I'm truly being me is when I can perceive that I'm firing on all cylinders. In other words, I'm truly being ME when I'm not shutting off any part of me.

The funny thing about that is when you truly have all of you showing up, playing small starts to be more and more difficult. When all cylinders are hot and firing, the things that used to stop you (judgment, projection, fear, rejection and all that) no longer carry the same blow, and allowance begins to come much quicker as well.

—*Sarah Grandinetti, USA*

Lisa Henriksson, Sweden

Whenever I wake up grumpy, I turn my head to look at a picture I keep beside my bed.

It's a picture of my daughter, Nova, on stage, beaming at me, her smile shining brighter than the sun itself, her hair wild, her outfit very, very casual.

Our family lives in Sweden, where most people share the point of view that you should never stick out or be different. It's better to be as normal as possible, to live your life in moderate balance.

Not Nova.

Whenever I look at that picture of my daughter, I'm reminded of how amazing it is — the way she deeply trusts that *being her* is extraordinary, brilliant in so many ways, how she knows on a deep level that being true to herself is much more important than fitting in. It's what truly matters.

The picture was taken many years ago when Nova had spent a week at her dad's house. That morning, he'd sent her off to school without remembering that that very evening she was going to be in a big show in the school assembly hall for all the parents.

When I got to the school, I saw her on stage in an outfit that looked like her pajamas and hair that hadn't seen a brush in days. She was definitely "sticking out."

If this had happened a few years ago, I would have felt extremely uncomfortable. I would have been seriously annoyed at my ex-husband for forgetting this important event in our daughter's world. I would have felt sorry for Nova and deeply embarrassed in front of all the other parents and teachers.

But that night, even though I was acutely aware of some of the other parents' judgments of our little untidy ray of sunshine, it didn't bother me in the least. From my new point of view, Nova's outfit, or anybody else's opinion of her or of me as a mother, wasn't a problem. Those opinions belonged to neither Nova nor me.

And apparently, Nova's very untidy hair and very abnormal outfit didn't matter to her either. I could see her beaming at me from the stage, and I thoroughly enjoyed the amazing show without worry.

In the car on the way home, sitting next to me, Nova looked so happy and pleased. Then suddenly, she said, "*Mom, Ellen said I was weird for not wearing my best clothes to the show, like all the other kids.*" I was about to ask her how she felt about that, but she had more to say. "*I told Ellen, 'It doesn't matter what I wear or what I look like. I know I'm wonderful and pretty just the way I am!'*"

My wise, magical, beautiful child had chosen one of the most rewarding attitudes I believe one can have: knowing you're brilliant and beautiful regardless of what anybody else thinks or says, and regardless of what you look like or what you do.

Nobody can take that away from you.

That night in the car, my heart melted. I felt so grateful my daughter didn't—and still doesn't—buy into the mandatory mediocrity and false security of being normal, of not standing out, of blending in.

It's so cool that she doesn't pick up and internalize everybody else's judgments and projections, as I did at her age, and for way too many years after. She is who she is, and she likes herself regardless. How does it get more beautiful than that?

If I had to choose between tangle free hair and Nova's love for who she is, I'd choose the love any day. *With that love, that light, that trust, what else is possible?*

Whenever I would like to "find myself" again, the easiest and quickest way is for me to start singing or listening to music, or just moving my body, which creates this connection and a level of presence with my body where I just know I am being me again.

—Marja Zapušek, Slovenia

Katarina Wallentin, Sweden

Most children are like walking talking radio receivers! They pick up on everything and are extremely (irritatingly) aware of what goes on around them, spoken or unspoken. And in contrast to all of us, children have not yet learned to pretend like nothing is different when the energy shifts or the mood swings.

My daughter knows within a split second if I have something going on. She will walk into my room and ask, *"Mum, is everything ok?"*

In that moment I can choose to be perfect or I can choose to be me. And my choice will give my daughter different gifts for the future.

Let's explore just two possible answers in a situation where I've have had an unexpected phone call that made me upset.

My daughter walks through the door and asks, *"Mum, is everything ok?"*

Alternative 1:
I answer, *"Oh yes, of course! Everything is fine, sweetie."*

Alternative 2:
I answer, *"I am a just bit upset. I just had a phone call with a friend of mine who gave me some news that made me really angry."*

Now, if I choose alternative one, my daughter will walk away doubting herself. She will stop trusting that gut feeling that is such an amazing guide in life. She will doubt her knowing and her capacity to read people and situations.

If I instead choose the second alternative, and choose to lower my barriers and be vulnerable with my daughter and with what is actually going on, that will acknowledge her awareness and knowing, and she will end up trusting herself even more in the future.

She will know that she knows.

In addition, it will open up the space of vulnerability for her. It'll show her that everything is allowed and included in our conversation.

Next time I ask her, *"Sweetie, are you ok?"* she will know it is ok to pull her barriers down as well, and answer with what is, and not with what is expected.

See, most of us spend our whole lives trying to say what is expected, normal and rational. We constantly try to prove how good and right we are, while thinking we're bad and wrong inside.

We learn early on to shut out that radio-receiver, since we doubt the energetic information we receive. And once the barriers are up, we can't even hear ourselves anymore.

Vulnerability can open up a completely new way to navigate the world—from your knowing. To have vulnerability with yourself is to never put up a barrier to who you truly are, or what is going on around you. That allows you to be present with everything, and be anything.

The thing is, you can't teach your children vulnerability.

The only way to give your child the gift of vulnerability is to be it.

Yes, there may definitively be times when it is appropriate to not tell a child exactly what is going on. There are times when what will create the most is to use a white lie in order to create the sense of safety that is required.

And you know when those times are. Those are not the times I am talking about. I am talking about all the other times.

Next time your child asks, *"Mum, Is Everything Ok?"* what if you choose to go for the vulnerable answer? **And be you.**

When I realized I was no longer choosing to filter the choices I was making in my life to please others. It was freeing beyond words.

—*Victoria Hickman, Australia*

"THERE ARE TW
YOU CAN LIVE
A MIRACLE; YO
EVERYTHING

O WAYS TO LIVE;
S IF NOTHING IS
CAN LIVE AS IF
S A MIRACLE."

—Albert Einstein

Margit Krathwohl, Germany

I came to a point in my life where I did not want to try any other method or another technique to improve my life. I felt stuck with my limitations, and it seemed like I was not open for a change. Or so I thought . . .

Shortly after, I came across some interviews for a different modality online and, surprisingly, the things they talked about were exactly what I knew but had no words for. So, I chose to attend a class called, 5 Days to Change Your Life. Before class started, I remember thinking, *"My life better change or I am out of here!"*

A few weeks later, I was diagnosed with cancer. It was a shock to me, as I had never been ill before. I was convinced I could heal it myself. But the tumor in my body kept growing no matter what I did. By the time I was willing to go to the hospital, the doctors told me they couldn't do anything for me, except to ease the pain.

I realized at that moment I had to make a choice.

As it was the weekend, I had two days to think about it without much action around me. Either I would die (and take another body) or I could keep this body (which I loved) and live.

The key thing for me was that I was apart from family and everybody I knew. I was able to make this choice just for me, without being the effect of all the projections, expectations and judgments from others.

And I made a choice. I am sure it was actually the first true choice for me being me I had ever made up till that point.

I chose to live! I chose to have the phenomenal life I never had before and to be happy! I talked with my body, *"Okay, I will do everything that is required for your healing."* With that choice, I was willing to be and do whatever it would take for my body to get well.

What then occurred was like a rollercoaster. In the hospital, unexpected operations and treatments suddenly had to be done in which they were able to remove the tumor — something that supposedly did not seem possible before.

Life has been an exciting journey ever since. It has given me a sense of peace, and a willingness to receive all those energies I had rejected before, that I wasn't even aware of before.Receiving everything, judging nothing, finally gives me a sense of ease and makes it so much more fun to be me!

I know I'm being me when no matter what is going on around me, I have space and ease and clarity. I know I'm being me when I'm happy. I know I'm being me when my life is in motion and when I perceive the timbre in my body, resonating with the people and things and earth around me.

I know I'm being me when I make a choice, especially when I say "yes" to something I haven't been willing to choose before. I know I'm being me when I'm being with someone, and their world changes, and my world changes.

—Kristen Tromble, Alaska

Peony Chung, Hong Kong

It is said that in the face of gratitude, judgment cannot survive or sustain. It is true.

When I was younger, I was told that I did not have gratitude for anything in my life. I spent 18 years trying to fix myself. I desperately tried to make myself good enough and to be more grateful, all according to other people's opinions and judgments of me.

I was so unhappy, and I was becoming aware that I had trapped myself in a tiny reality my whole life. Eventually, I reached a tipping point; I created a demand to either change it or die.

One night shortly after, I was reading the book, *Being You, Changing the World*, by Dr. Dain Heer, and it asked: "IN WHICH THREE SITUATIONS HAVE YOU EVER HAD A STRONG SENSE

OF TRULY BEING YOU?"

It brought me back to the moment when my dad had died a few years earlier.

This was after my mother had committed suicide and all the trauma, sadness and emotions that followed in my family. Basically, my dad and I had spent our entire lives struggling to set things right without success.

It was not until he had been lying on his deathbed for 24 hours — when his mind could not function anymore, but his body still had sensation and could hear me — that he finally could receive me with no judgment at all.

Finally, everyone there, including my father, had a sense of peace, allowance, gratitude, vulnerability and honor.

That was the first moment in my life that I was seen and received as me, while not being judged at all by my family.

So, there I was, reading the book and realizing that I had a concept of what being you could be like — even if it doesn't have a solid form or can be figured out.

I was so grateful. I cried and cried, and my body released all the charge locked up for so many years.

It is a never-ending journey, being.

No one can tell me 'how' to move on with my life, including me. In fact, I have to get out of my own way.

Choice is the key. I have learned to keep choosing and keep demanding to be me, no matter what. No one can tell me what to do or how to do it. It is only when I choose, that the door opens.

When I don't have to pretend or try to align with any situation, when I am truly being me instead of someone I am supposed to be, and when I don't have to make an effort and it comes out easily. Then I truly know that I am being me.

—Ayla Aydin, Turkey

"TODAY IS

FUL DAY.

SEEN IT

—Maya Angelou

Wendy Mulder, Australia

When we get caught up or consumed with grief, it can feel impossible to believe there is something greater beyond it. What if the key to recovering from grief is rediscovering you? And yet, even the simplest shift in our point of view can allow us a level of peace, ease, possibility, and even magic, that we never before believed could be available.

When I chose to be more of me in care giving for my dying mother, I started to create, with ease, what many people believe impossible in those situations.

What showed up from being willing to constantly ask for greater possibility and being vulnerable and honest about what I desired and required to choose, was that I was able to create every moment, every choice, every "obstacle" as a gift and a possibility, rather than a problem.

I also got to receive the joy of contributing to my mother and being grateful for her in my life while still being engaged with my daily living. Being me allowed me to choose care-giving without having the 'burn-out', exhaustion or the overwhelm that often stops us from being able to be present, aware and able to receive all that is available with ease.

What if we could see grief from a space of allowance, question, and possibility?

I am truly grateful for the gift that caring for my mother was in my life and the lives of my family. What could have been trauma and long-standing grief became an awareness of the gift that every choice brings and the lies of loss that we do not need to buy.

If grief was a gift, what choices could it offer you, and what changes could those choices bring?

My favorite tool to come back to myself is connecting with the earth.

If I have time, I prefer to spend it in nature. If I am busy and it has to be now, this very moment is all it takes to connect with the earth. I can do this anywhere; at home between activities or in the middle of the city.

The earth is always just underneath, and even the house, the concrete or pavement are made from materials that come from the earth. I just have to close my eyes and remember a time in the deep forest, in the mountains, on the beach or in the desert that was special.

Boom!

The connection is there, and I move back to being me.

—*Corinna Stoeffl, Germany*

Katarina Wallentin, Sweden

Recently, my mum died of cancer.

When she passed, my dad, my brother and I sat with her for the last six hours, being present with every single shallow cumbersome breath; in and out, in and out.

Each of those last breaths were suddenly so precious, after all those hundreds of thousands upon hundreds of thousands of breaths that naturally had flowed through her body during her whole life, never really reflected over, never really noticed.

We said, *"It is all good, it is all taken care of, you can leave now, you're ready."*

In and out.

In and out.

We said, *"It is all well, we're taken care of, you can leave now, we're ready."*

In and out.

In and out.

And there was nothing required in that room, except **being**.

Roles, relationships, agendas, projections, expectations, separations and lies...it all fell away.

We existed in a space that stretched far beyond that room, and far beyond that moment in time. And as the last rays of the summer evening sun moved across her face, my mother finally left. A last slow hesitant breath and then only the body remained, like a white empty fragile shell.

In that moment, it was scorchingly clear to me that we, as beings, **are vibrations of energy.** We are an acoustic wave that for a short period rocks and moves and dances with, and within, a body.

I will always miss my mother's way of dancing. And my dance will be forever changed by those hours in that room.

Being me, in that room, at the hospice, those hours with my mum's last breaths... that was EASY. **In that room, only being could exist.**

Being me, the weeks after she passed; planning for the memorial service, sorting papers, meeting friends and relatives and neighbors; that was a much greater challenge.

Every day I asked, "*If I was being me right now,* WHO *would I be?*"

And I kept breathing.

In and out.

In and out.

Every day I asked, "*If I was being me right now,* WHAT *would I be?*"

And I kept breathing.

In and out.

In and out.

Every day I asked, "*If I was being me right now,* HOW *would I be?*"

And I kept dancing.

In and out.

In and out.

With time, it got easier.

This I know: I *be* a new dance every day. Sometimes it is GLORIOUS, sometimes funny and sometimes hesitant, or even sloppy.

But every dance is precious.

BEING YOU,
BEING PRESENT

HOW DO YOU KNOW WHEN YOU'RE BEING YOU?

The moments I know I am being me, my hair could stand up from the excitement of being alive, and at that same time there is a relaxation and peace throughout my whole world.

I know that I am being and doing what truly brings me joy - whether it's jumping out of a plane, landing in a new country ready for an adventure, or spending the day exploring nature with my children.

—Emily Evans Russell, USA

"YOU'RE NO

FOLLOW. YOU

BE THAT WH

T HERE TO

ARE HERE TO

CH INSPIRES."

—Dain Heer

Pragya Sabine Erlei, Germany

Losing everything, I had no other choice than to just be me.

A few years ago everything had fallen apart, and I really had no clue what to do or where to go next.

I was hiding in a room, so no one would see my tears. And then a friend found me there and invited me to sit with her while I was crying, so she could hold me.

After a little while, still lost in my tears from all the seemingly terrible things that had occurred in my life, my friend looked at me and said, *"You look so beautiful in your tears, your face is gorgeous."*

I said, sobbing, *"Me, beautiful? Now? I feel so ugly! How can I be beautiful in all of this?"* I had so much judgment of me and the world.

Some years later, I finally got what she meant.

By then I had seen people, lost in that same space, with their illusions of their perfect worlds breaking down, and that was exactly the moment when they were actually truly being themselves.

What appeared to them to be the end of the world allowed them to be divinely, humbly uniquely, brilliantly true to themselves. There was an innocence and vulnerability in those moments that were beautiful — it opened my heart immediately and allowed me to just be present.

I know many of us don't like to cry. What if it is just the water of life flowing again, where it has been stuck and stagnant?

I encourage you never to judge your crying. Don't try to stop it. Let it flow, and then choose what you would like to do next.

Your tears may be even more beautiful than your laughter and everything else you try to impress the world with. Your tears may show you what is true for you in that moment, and show you the next step on your way.

What if we fall together, not apart?

HOW DO YOU KNOW WHEN YOU'RE BEING YOU?

I know I am being me when I'm at peace with anything I do, be and say.

There is no doubt, there is lightness, and a sense of space, where I don't have to define anything.

—Norma Forestiere, Brazil

"TO BE YOURSE

THAT IS CONST

MAKE YOU INTO S

THE GREATEST A

F IN A WORLD

NTLY TRYING TO

METHING ELSE IS

COMPLISHMENT."

—RALPH WALDO EMERSON

First time I discovered I was being me was the moment I jumped out of an airplane, and I was not nervous at all.

Every step of preparing for and actually skydiving was pure joy and excitement, and as soon as we landed on the ground, I wanted to go and do it again.

I realized I really do not have any fears, and if anything, I was able to acknowledge how much I love speed and the exploration of most things that people "fear".

—Laleh Hancock, USA

Kristen Tromble, Alaska

I am being me, being here, and being present.

I listen, ask a question, and sometimes just continue to sit quietly as someone tells me about a relationship that is ending badly. Someone else tells me about their tastes in porn; someone tells me about struggling with the conflict between their love for a relative who is gay and their belief that being gay is wrong; someone tells me of being accused of child abuse, being convicted and in jail; someone tells me of the time they knew of a plan to kill someone and made sure they were somewhere else, but did nothing to stop it; someone tells me of the times they've killed someone; someone tells me they shot their dog; someone tells me they'd like to die.

I have no training as a counselor.

I just have the space to be, as people tell me things they never thought they'd tell anyone. And with that telling in that space, a heaviness lifts.

There's space for them and me, for us, to perceive that the action, the emotion, the thought, the "horrible" thing that they defined as their irrevocable wrongness is truly NOT who they be.

It doesn't have to define them for the rest of their life. It really doesn't have to define them at all.

They can choose to be and create themselves as something different.

Perhaps they can even be that space for someone else in the future who will tell them something "horrible" that no longer needs to define them.

The space of peace that nature, children and animals offer allows me to connect on a cellular, molecular level to the intricate simplicity of life, and invites me to remember who I am.

I spend a few moments marveling at how easily the cells and molecules come together through nature to create the complexity of a rose. I'm intrigued by the cat who stops mid-step to look and listen attentively to even the slightest movement in the grass.

My whole body immediately begins to relax when I do that. My breathing changes, my heartbeat finds its rhythm and all of a sudden, I am me again.

A soft, perhaps invisible smile breaks out on my face; my jaw bone loosens up, my forehead un-furrows (and my brain with it).

Things start to get clearer and gentler in my world. All worries fill up with this space of ease, and I begin to laugh to myself. Hahahaha, I'm back. I start being me again, and I know with certainty that everything truly is possible.

—*Kass Thomas, Italy*

YOUR CHECKLIST
FOR BEING

TAKE ANOTHER STEP

Here we are, at the very end of this exploration of creating you, choosing and being you.

Before we say good bye, I would like to gift you a reminder, a way to know when you are being you . . .

A checklist . . . for being.

1. You like yourself.

2. You care about the people around you. A lot. Whatever they choose.

3. There is no awareness you have to avoid — the good, the bad and the ugly. Everything fits in your world. You can be totally present with everything and everyone.

4. You have a dynamic sense of peace. (You may still be potent enough to start a tsunami of change with your little finger!)

5. You're magic walking, with every step, something new and wondrous is added to the symphony of possibilities.

6. You're continuously changing!

That is, you. That is your check list.

Now, if you're not there right now, that is okay! I totally get how sometimes it seems so difficult to be here and put one foot in front of another and take the next step.

Make no mistake about it, I experience that too. It doesn't mean you're wrong—or not getting consciousness. It is part of this journey, and part of why so few people are choosing it.

Here is the thing: Right now, you and your choices, and we and the choices we are making together, are creating a new space where it will be easier for everyone coming after us.

You, my friend, just by asking to Be You, are at the creative edge of this reality and of consciousness. You are, right now, one of the most courageous people on this planet.

Please know that. Never give up. Be you in the moment and choose from there. Take another step. And another. And another.

And remember, you're a continuous creation. There is nothing finite about you. You don't have to "find you", there is nothing to find. Your mission, should you choose to accept it, is to create you as you truly be.

Are you in? What if you are the difference the Earth has been waiting for?

—Dain Heer,
Houston, Texas USA

CUT OUT AND PUT ON YOUR FRIDGE...

YOUR CHECKLIST FOR BEING

By Dain Heer

1. *You like yourself.*

2. *You care about the people around you. A lot. Whatever they choose.*

3. *There is no awareness you have to avoid — the good, the bad and the ugly. Everything fits in your world. You can be totally present with everything and everyone.*

4. *You have a dynamic sense of peace. (You may still be potent enough to start a tsunami of change with your little finger!)*

5. *You're magic walking, with every step, something new and wondrous is added to the symphony of possibilities.*

6. *You're continuously changing!*

CPSIA information can be obtained
at www.ICGtesting.com
Printed in the USA
BVHW092226120819
555663BV00023B/2133/P

9 781634 932806